D1797934

ISBN:9781087858845

This Journal belongs to:

How to use this Journal?

In this journal, you can reflect on your day and write your thoughts down. You can keep track of your day to day activities such as practices, projects, and assignments. This journal is ALL yours.

What is Journaling?

Journaling is simply putting your thoughts and feelings on paper.

▲

What are the benefits Journaling?

Journaling is a healthy way of expressing and processing big emotions.

▲

In fact, even the hairs on your head are all numbered. Do not be afraid; you are more valuable than many sparrows.

Luke 12:7

ALL ABOUT ME

Sports that I play:

My Favorite Number is:

My Dream Job:

My Hobbies are:

Dream

PLAN

GROW

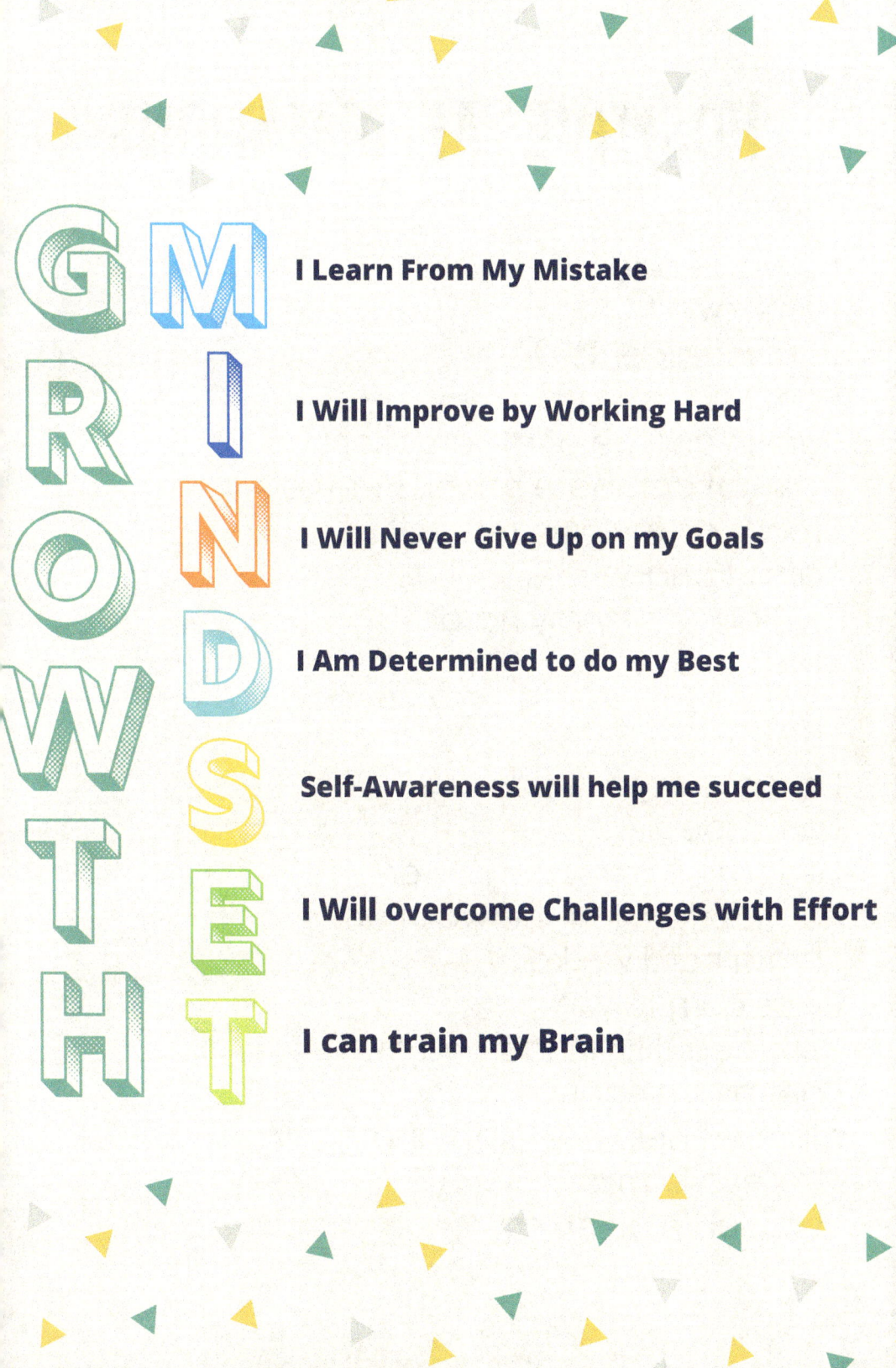

GROWTH MINDSET

I Learn From My Mistake

I Will Improve by Working Hard

I Will Never Give Up on my Goals

I Am Determined to do my Best

Self-Awareness will help me succeed

I Will overcome Challenges with Effort

I can train my Brain

POSITIVE AFFIRMATIONS

I am a Leader
I am Loved
I am Intelligent
I am ME
I am in charge of my emotions
I will not compare myself to others
I focus on my own result
I am Strong
I will always try my hardest

I choose my Attitude
I am Obedient
Learning is my superpower
I am perfect just the way I am
I am a hard worker
I was born to win
I am beautiful inside and out
I am brave enough to try
Mistakes help me learn and grow
I believe in myself
I can learn anything

3 THINGS I LOVE ABOUT MYSELF!

1 _____

2 _____

3 _____

MONTHLY GOALS

JANUARY

_____
_____
_____

FEBRUARY

_____
_____
_____

MARCH

_____
_____
_____

APRIL

_____
_____
_____

MAY

_____
_____
_____

JUNE

_____
_____
_____

JULY

_____
_____
_____

AUGUST

_____
_____
_____

SEPTEMBER

_____
_____
_____

OCTOBER

_____
_____
_____

NOVEMBER

_____
_____
_____

DECEMBER

_____
_____
_____

HOMEWORK

TO DO LIST

MONDAY

_____

_____

_____

TUESDAY

_____

_____

_____

WEDNESDAY

_____

_____

_____

REMINDERS

THURSDAY

_____

_____

_____

_____

FRIDAY

_____

_____

_____

HOMEWORK

MONDAY

_____
_____
_____

TUESDAY

_____
_____
_____

WEDNESDAY

_____
_____
_____

THURSDAY

_____
_____
_____

FRIDAY

_____
_____
_____

TO DO LIST

_____
_____
_____
_____
_____
_____
_____
_____
_____

REMINDERS

_____
_____
_____
_____
_____
_____
_____
_____
_____
_____

PROJECTS AND EXAMS

Description

Deadline

Class

Important Days

_____

Details

_____
_____

_____

_____
_____

Complete

Description

Deadline

Class

Important Days

_____

Details

_____
_____

_____

_____
_____

Complete

Description

Deadline

Class

Important Days

_____

Details

_____
_____

_____

_____
_____

Complete

My Mood Tracker

Month _____

Today I Felt...

Energetic/Motivated Happy Content/Neutral

Sad Anxious Irritable/Annoyed Angry Sick/Tired

Date: / /

DAILY PLANNER

MORNING MUST

☐ Shower and dress
☐ Quiet time
☐ Reading

_____
_____

TO DO LIST

Calls
_____

Texts
_____

CHORES

MORNING	AFTERNOON	EVENING

A LITTLE TIME FOR ME

_____
_____

EXERCISE 🚲

WATER 🥛

BREAKFAST	LUNCH	DINNER

SPECIAL MEMORY OF THE DAY

_____
_____
_____
_____

DAILY PLANNER

MORNING MUST

☐ Shower and dress

☐ Quiet time

☐ Reading

_____

_____

TO DO LIST

Calls

_____

Texts

_____

CHORES

MORNING	AFTERNOON	EVENING

A LITTLE TIME FOR ME

_____

_____

EXERCISE 🚲

WATER 🪣

BREAKFAST	LUNCH	DINNER

SPECIAL MEMORY OF THE DAY

_____

_____

_____

_____

DAILY PLANNER

MORNING MUST

☐ Shower and dress

☐ Quiet time

☐ Reading

_____

_____

TO DO LIST

Calls
_____

Texts
_____

CHORES

MORNING	AFTERNOON	EVENING

A LITTLE TIME FOR ME

_____

_____

EXERCISE 🚲

WATER 🥛

BREAKFAST	LUNCH	DINNER

SPECIAL MEMORY OF THE DAY

_____

_____

_____

_____

DAILY PLANNER

MORNING MUST

☐ Shower and dress
☐ Quiet time
☐ Reading

_____
_____

TO DO LIST

Calls
_____

Texts
_____

CHORES

MORNING	AFTERNOON	EVENING

A LITTLE TIME FOR ME

_____
_____

EXERCISE 🚲

WATER 🥛

BREAKFAST	LUNCH	DINNER

SPECIAL MEMORY OF THE DAY

_____
_____
_____
_____

DAILY PLANNER

MORNING MUST

☐ Shower and dress

☐ Quiet time

☐ Reading

_____

_____

TO DO LIST

Calls

_____

Texts

_____

CHORES

MORNING	AFTERNOON	EVENING

A LITTLE TIME FOR ME

_____

_____

EXERCISE 🚲

WATER 🥛

BREAKFAST	LUNCH	DINNER

SPECIAL MEMORY OF THE DAY

_____

_____

_____

_____

DAILY PLANNER

MORNING MUST

- ☐ Shower and dress
- ☐ Quiet time
- ☐ Reading

_____

_____

TO DO LIST

Calls
_____

Texts
_____

CHORES

MORNING	AFTERNOON	EVENING

A LITTLE TIME FOR ME

_____

_____

EXERCISE 🚲

WATER 🥛

BREAKFAST	LUNCH	DINNER

SPECIAL MEMORY OF THE DAY

_____

_____

_____

_____

Date: / /

DAILY PLANNER

MORNING MUST	TO DO LIST	CHORES

MORNING MUST
☐ Shower and dress
☐ Quiet time
☐ Reading
_____
_____

Calls
_____

Texts
_____

MORNING	AFTERNOON	EVENING

A LITTLE TIME FOR ME	BREAKFAST	LUNCH	DINNER

A LITTLE TIME FOR ME
_____
_____

EXERCISE 🚲

WATER 🥤

SPECIAL MEMORY OF THE DAY
_____
_____
_____
_____

DAILY PLANNER

MORNING MUST

☐ Shower and dress
☐ Quiet time
☐ Reading

_____
_____

TO DO LIST

Calls
_____
Texts
_____

CHORES

MORNING	AFTERNOON	EVENING

A LITTLE TIME FOR ME

_____
_____

EXERCISE 🚲

WATER ⬜

BREAKFAST	LUNCH	DINNER

SPECIAL MEMORY OF THE DAY

_____
_____
_____
_____

DAILY PLANNER

MORNING MUST

☐ Shower and dress

☐ Quiet time

☐ Reading

_____

_____

TO DO LIST

Calls
_____

Texts
_____

CHORES

MORNING	AFTERNOON	EVENING

A LITTLE TIME FOR ME

_____

_____

EXERCISE 🚲

WATER 🥛

BREAKFAST	LUNCH	DINNER

SPECIAL MEMORY OF THE DAY

_____

_____

_____

_____

DAILY PLANNER

MORNING MUST

☐ Shower and dress

☐ Quiet time

☐ Reading

_____

_____

TO DO LIST

Calls
_____

Texts
_____

CHORES

MORNING	AFTERNOON	EVENING

A LITTLE TIME FOR ME

_____

_____

EXERCISE 🚲

WATER 🪣

BREAKFAST	LUNCH	DINNER

SPECIAL MEMORY OF THE DAY

_____

_____

_____

_____

My Mood Tracker

Month _____

Today I Felt...

Dates around circle: 31, 1, 2, 3, 4, 5, 6, 7, 8, 9, 10, 11, 12, 13, 14, 15, 16, 17, 18, 19, 20, 21, 22, 23, 24, 25, 26, 27, 28, 29, 30

Energetic/Motivated

Happy

Content/Neutral

Sad

Anxious

Irritable/Annoyed

Angry

Sick/Tired

DAILY PLANNER

MORNING MUST

☐ Shower and dress
☐ Quiet time
☐ Reading

_____
_____

TO DO LIST

Calls
_____

Texts
_____

CHORES

MORNING	AFTERNOON	EVENING

A LITTLE TIME FOR ME

_____
_____

EXERCISE 🚲

WATER 🥛

BREAKFAST	LUNCH	DINNER

SPECIAL MEMORY OF THE DAY

_____
_____
_____
_____

DAILY PLANNER

MORNING MUST

- ☐ Shower and dress
- ☐ Quiet time
- ☐ Reading
- _____
- _____

TO DO LIST

Calls
_____

Texts
_____

CHORES

MORNING	AFTERNOON	EVENING

A LITTLE TIME FOR ME

_____

_____

EXERCISE 🚲

WATER 🥛

BREAKFAST	LUNCH	DINNER

SPECIAL MEMORY OF THE DAY

_____

_____

_____

_____

DAILY PLANNER

MORNING MUST

☐ Shower and dress
☐ Quiet time
☐ Reading

_____

_____

TO DO LIST

Calls
_____

Texts
_____

CHORES

MORNING	AFTERNOON	EVENING

A LITTLE TIME FOR ME

_____

_____

EXERCISE 🚲

WATER 🥛

BREAKFAST	LUNCH	DINNER

SPECIAL MEMORY OF THE DAY

_____

_____

_____

_____

DAILY PLANNER

MORNING MUST

☐ Shower and dress

☐ Quiet time

☐ Reading

_____

_____

TO DO LIST

Calls

_____

Texts

_____

CHORES

MORNING	AFTERNOON	EVENING

A LITTLE TIME FOR ME

_____

_____

EXERCISE 🚲

WATER 🥛

BREAKFAST	LUNCH	DINNER

SPECIAL MEMORY OF THE DAY

_____

_____

_____

_____

DAILY PLANNER

MORNING MUST

☐ Shower and dress
☐ Quiet time
☐ Reading
_____
_____

TO DO LIST

Calls
_____

Texts
_____

CHORES

MORNING	AFTERNOON	EVENING

A LITTLE TIME FOR ME

_____
_____

EXERCISE 🚲

WATER 🥤

BREAKFAST	LUNCH	DINNER

SPECIAL MEMORY OF THE DAY

_____
_____
_____
_____

DAILY PLANNER

MORNING MUST

☐ Shower and dress

☐ Quiet time

☐ Reading

_____

_____

TO DO LIST

Calls
_____

Texts
_____

CHORES

MORNING	AFTERNOON	EVENING

A LITTLE TIME FOR ME

_____

_____

EXERCISE 🚲

WATER 🥛

BREAKFAST	LUNCH	DINNER

SPECIAL MEMORY OF THE DAY

_____

_____

_____

_____

DAILY PLANNER

MORNING MUST

☐ Shower and dress
☐ Quiet time
☐ Reading

_____
_____

TO DO LIST

Calls
_____

Texts
_____

CHORES

MORNING	AFTERNOON	EVENING

A LITTLE TIME FOR ME

_____
_____

EXERCISE 🚲

WATER 🥛

BREAKFAST	LUNCH	DINNER

SPECIAL MEMORY OF THE DAY

_____
_____
_____
_____

My Mood Tracker

Month _____

Today I Felt...

Energetic/Motivated

Happy

Content/Neutral

Sad

Anxious

Irritable/Annoyed

Angry

Sick/Tired

DAILY PLANNER

MORNING MUST

☐ Shower and dress

☐ Quiet time

☐ Reading

_____

_____

TO DO LIST

Calls

Texts

CHORES

MORNING	AFTERNOON	EVENING

A LITTLE TIME FOR ME

_____

_____

EXERCISE 🚲

WATER 🥛

BREAKFAST	LUNCH	DINNER

SPECIAL MEMORY OF THE DAY

_____

_____

_____

_____

Date: / /

DAILY PLANNER

☐ Shower and dress

☐ Quiet time

☐ Reading

_____

_____

TO DO LIST

Calls
_____

Texts
_____

CHORES

MORNING	AFTERNOON	EVENING

A LITTLE TIME FOR ME

_____

_____

EXERCISE 🚲

WATER 🥛

BREAKFAST	LUNCH	DINNER

SPECIAL MEMORY OF THE DAY

_____

_____

_____

_____

DAILY PLANNER

MORNING MUST

☐ Shower and dress
☐ Quiet time
☐ Reading

_____

_____

TO DO LIST

Calls
_____

Texts
_____

CHORES

MORNING	AFTERNOON	EVENING

A LITTLE TIME FOR ME

_____

_____

EXERCISE 🚲

WATER 🥤

BREAKFAST	LUNCH	DINNER

SPECIAL MEMORY OF THE DAY

_____

_____

_____

_____

DAILY PLANNER

MORNING MUST

☐ Shower and dress

☐ Quiet time

☐ Reading

_____

_____

TO DO LIST

Calls
_____

Texts
_____

CHORES

MORNING	AFTERNOON	EVENING

A LITTLE TIME FOR ME

_____

_____

EXERCISE 🚲

WATER 🥛

BREAKFAST	LUNCH	DINNER

SPECIAL MEMORY OF THE DAY

_____

_____

_____

_____

DAILY PLANNER

MORNING MUST	TO DO LIST	CHORES
☐ Shower and dress		
☐ Quiet time		
☐ Reading	Calls	
_____		
_____	Texts	

MORNING	AFTERNOON	EVENING

A LITTLE TIME FOR ME	BREAKFAST	LUNCH	DINNER
_____			
_____			
EXERCISE 🚲			
WATER 🥛			

SPECIAL MEMORY OF THE DAY

_____

_____

_____

_____

Date: / /

DAILY PLANNER

MORNING MUST
☐ Shower and dress
☐ Quiet time
☐ Reading
_____
_____

TO DO LIST

Calls
_____
Texts
_____

CHORES

MORNING	AFTERNOON	EVENING

A LITTLE TIME FOR ME
_____
_____

EXERCISE 🚲

WATER 🥛

BREAKFAST	LUNCH	DINNER

SPECIAL MEMORY OF THE DAY
_____
_____
_____
_____

DAILY PLANNER

MORNING MUST

☐ Shower and dress
☐ Quiet time
☐ Reading

_____
_____

TO DO LIST

Calls
_____

Texts
_____

CHORES

MORNING	AFTERNOON	EVENING

A LITTLE TIME FOR ME

_____
_____

EXERCISE 🚲

WATER 🪣

BREAKFAST	LUNCH	DINNER

SPECIAL MEMORY OF THE DAY

_____
_____
_____
_____

My Mood Tracker

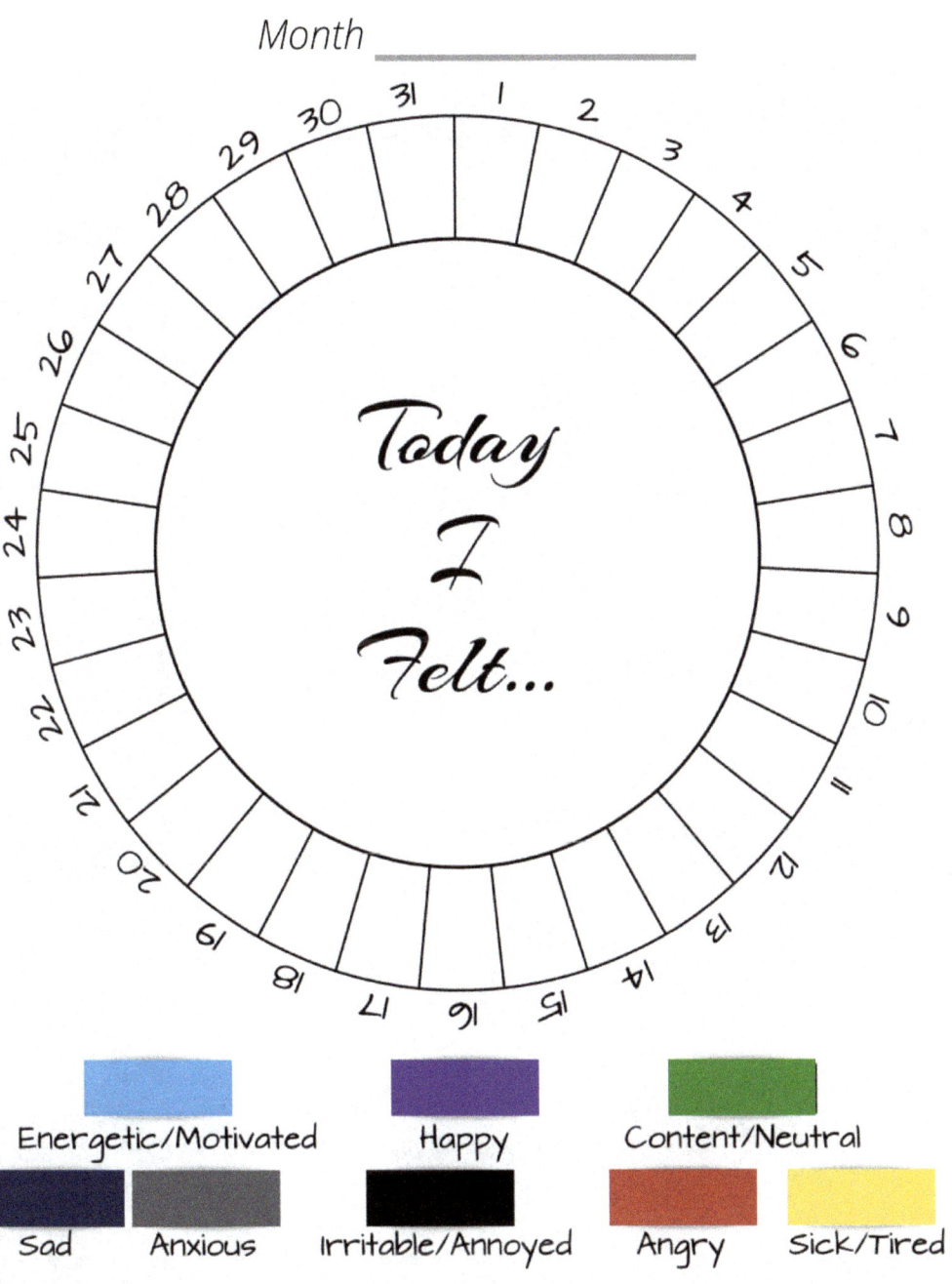

Today I Felt...

31 1 2 3 4 5 6 7 8 9 10 11 12 13 14 15 16 17 18 19 20 21 22 23 24 25 26 27 28 29 30

Energetic/Motivated

Happy

Content/Neutral

Sad

Anxious

Irritable/Annoyed

Angry

Sick/Tired

Date: / /

DAILY PLANNER

MORNING MUST
☐ Shower and dress
☐ Quiet time
☐ Reading
_____
_____

TO DO LIST

Calls
_____

Texts

CHORES

MORNING	AFTERNOON	EVENING

A LITTLE TIME FOR ME
_____
_____

EXERCISE 🚲

WATER 🪣

BREAKFAST	LUNCH	DINNER

SPECIAL MEMORY OF THE DAY
_____
_____
_____
_____

Date: / /

DAILY PLANNER

MORNING MUST

☐ Shower and dress

☐ Quiet time

☐ Reading

_____

_____

TO DO LIST

Calls
_____

Texts
_____

CHORES

MORNING	AFTERNOON	EVENING

A LITTLE TIME FOR ME

_____

_____

EXERCISE 🚲

WATER 🥛

BREAKFAST	LUNCH	DINNER

SPECIAL MEMORY OF THE DAY

_____

_____

_____

_____

DAILY PLANNER

MORNING MUST

☐ Shower and dress

☐ Quiet time

☐ Reading

_____

_____

TO DO LIST

Calls

_____

Texts

_____

CHORES

MORNING	AFTERNOON	EVENING

A LITTLE TIME FOR ME

_____

_____

EXERCISE 🚲

WATER 🥛

BREAKFAST	LUNCH	DINNER

SPECIAL MEMORY OF THE DAY

_____

_____

_____

_____

DAILY PLANNER

MORNING MUST

☐ Shower and dress

☐ Quiet time

☐ Reading

_____

_____

TO DO LIST

Calls

_____

Texts

_____

CHORES

MORNING	AFTERNOON	EVENING

A LITTLE TIME FOR ME

_____

_____

EXERCISE 🚲

WATER 🥛

BREAKFAST	LUNCH	DINNER

SPECIAL MEMORY OF THE DAY

_____

_____

_____

_____

DAILY PLANNER

MORNING MUST

☐ Shower and dress
☐ Quiet time
☐ Reading

_____

_____

TO DO LIST

Calls

_____

Texts

_____

CHORES

MORNING	AFTERNOON	EVENING

A LITTLE TIME FOR ME

_____

_____

EXERCISE 🚲

WATER 🥛

BREAKFAST	LUNCH	DINNER

SPECIAL MEMORY OF THE DAY

_____

_____

_____

_____

Date: //

DAILY PLANNER

MORNING MUST

☐ Shower and dress

☐ Quiet time

☐ Reading

_____

_____

TO DO LIST

Calls

Texts

CHORES

MORNING	AFTERNOON	EVENING

A LITTLE TIME FOR ME

_____

_____

EXERCISE 🚲

WATER 🥛

BREAKFAST	LUNCH	DINNER

SPECIAL MEMORY OF THE DAY

_____

_____

_____

_____

DAILY PLANNER

MORNING MUST

☐ Shower and dress
☐ Quiet time
☐ Reading

_____
_____

TO DO LIST

Calls
_____

Texts
_____

CHORES

MORNING	AFTERNOON	EVENING

A LITTLE TIME FOR ME

_____
_____

EXERCISE 🚲

WATER 🥤

BREAKFAST	LUNCH	DINNER

SPECIAL MEMORY OF THE DAY

_____
_____
_____
_____

Date: / /

DAILY PLANNER

MORNING MUST

☐ Shower and dress

☐ Quiet time

☐ Reading

_____

_____

TO DO LIST

Calls

_____

Texts

_____

CHORES

MORNING	AFTERNOON	EVENING

A LITTLE TIME FOR ME

_____

_____

EXERCISE

WATER

BREAKFAST	LUNCH	DINNER

SPECIAL MEMORY OF THE DAY

_____

_____

_____

_____

My Mood Tracker

Today I Felt...

Energetic/Motivated	Happy	Content/Neutral

Sad	Anxious	Irritable/Annoyed	Angry	Sick/Tired

TODAY IS: _____

6:00	
7:00	
8:00	
9:00	
10:00	
11:00	
12:00	
1:00	
2:00	
3:00	
4:00	
5:00	
6:00	
7:00	
8:00	
9:00	

ASSIGNMENTS

CHORES

NOTES

Date: / /

GRATITUDE JOURNAL

GRATITUDE MORNING
Before you begin your day, list 10 things you´re grateful for.

1 _____
2 _____
3 _____
4 _____
5 _____
6 _____
7 _____
8 _____
9 _____
10_____

WHAT I´M LEARNING FROM MY CHALLENGES
List three obstacles and what you´re learning from them.

1 What I´m learning:

2 What I´m learning:

3 What I´m learning:

PEOPLE I´M GRATEFUL FOR
List 5 people who made your life a little happier today. these could be friends, family or strangers.

1 _____
2 _____
3 _____
4 _____
5 _____

THE BEST PART OF MY DAY
Choose one moment of your day that made you happy and focus on it for 5 minutes before bed.

_____
_____
_____
_____
_____
_____
_____
_____

Date: / /

GRATITUDE JOURNAL

GRATITUDE MORNING

Before you begin your day, list 10 things you´re grateful for.

_____
_____
_____
_____
_____
_____
_____
_____
_____
_____
_____
_____

WHAT I´M LEARNING FROM MY CHALLENGES

List three obstacles and what you´re learning from them.

1 What I´m learning:

2 What I´m learning:

3 What I´m learning:

PEOPLE I´M GRATEFUL FOR

List 5 people who made your life a little happier today. these could be friends, family or strangers.

_____
_____
_____
_____
_____

THE BEST PART OF MY DAY

Choose one moment of your day that made you happy and focus on it for 5 minutes before bed.

_____
_____
_____
_____
_____
_____
_____
_____
_____

Date: / /

GRATITUDE JOURNAL

GRATITUDE MORNING
Before you begin your day, list 10 things you´re grateful for.

1 _____
2 _____
3 _____
4 _____
5 _____
6 _____
7 _____
8 _____
9 _____
10 _____

WHAT I´M LEARNING FROM MY CHALLENGES
List three obstacles and what you´re learning from them.

1 What I´m learning:

2 What I´m learning:

3 What I´m learning:

PEOPLE I´M GRATEFUL FOR
List 5 people who made your life a little happier today. these could be friends, family or strangers.

1 _____
2 _____
3 _____
4 _____
5 _____

THE BEST PART OF MY DAY
Choose one moment of your day that made you happy and focus on it for 5 minutes before bed.

_____
_____
_____
_____
_____
_____
_____
_____
_____

GRATITUDE JOURNAL

GRATITUDE MORNING

Before you begin your day, list 10
things you´re grateful for.

_____
_____
_____
_____
_____
_____
_____
_____
_____
_____

WHAT I´M LEARNING FROM MY CHALLENGES

List three obstacles and
what you´re learning from
them.

1 What I´m learning:

2 What I´m learning:

3 What I´m learning:

PEOPLE I´M GRATEFUL FOR

List 5 people who made your life a
little happier today. these could be
friends, family or strangers.

_____
_____
_____
_____
_____

THE BEST PART OF MY DAY

Choose one moment of your day
that made you happy and focus
on it for 5 minutes before bed.

_____
_____
_____
_____
_____
_____
_____
_____

Date: / /

GRATITUDE JOURNAL

GRATITUDE MORNING
Before you begin your day, list 10 things you´re grateful for.

1 _____
2 _____
3 _____
4 _____
5 _____
6 _____
7 _____
8 _____
9 _____
10 _____

WHAT I´M LEARNING FROM MY CHALLENGES
List three obstacles and what you´re learning from them.

1 What I´m learning:

2 What I´m learning:

3 What I´m learning:

PEOPLE I´M GRATEFUL FOR
List 5 people who made your life a little happier today. these could be friends, family or strangers.

1 _____
2 _____
3 _____
4 _____
5 _____

THE BEST PART OF MY DAY
Choose one moment of your day that made you happy and focus on it for 5 minutes before bed.

_____
_____
_____
_____
_____
_____
_____
_____
_____

Date: / /

GRATITUDE JOURNAL

GRATITUDE MORNING

Before you begin your day, list 10 things you´re grateful for.

_____
_____
_____
_____
_____
_____
_____
_____
_____
_____
_____
_____

WHAT I´M LEARNING FROM MY CHALLENGES

List three obstacles and what you´re learning from them.

1 What I´m learning:

2 What I´m learning:

3 What I´m learning:

PEOPLE I´M GRATEFUL FOR

List 5 people who made your life a little happier today. these could be friends, family or strangers.

_____
_____
_____
_____
_____

THE BEST PART OF MY DAY

Choose one moment of your day that made you happy and focus on it for 5 minutes before bed.

_____
_____
_____
_____
_____
_____
_____
_____

Date: / /

GRATITUDE JOURNAL

GRATITUDE MORNING

Before you begin your day, list 10 things you´re grateful for.

1 _____

2 _____

3 _____

4 _____

5 _____

6 _____

7 _____

8 _____

9 _____

10 _____

WHAT I´M LEARNING FROM MY CHALLENGES

List three obstacles and what you´re learning from them.

1 What I´m learning:

2 What I´m learning:

3 What I´m learning:

PEOPLE I´M GRATEFUL FOR

List 5 people who made your life a little happier today. these could be friends, family or strangers.

1 _____

2 _____

3 _____

4 _____

5 _____

THE BEST PART OF MY DAY

Choose one moment of your day that made you happy and focus on it for 5 minutes before bed.

_____

_____

_____

_____

_____

_____

_____

_____

Date: / /

GRATITUDE JOURNAL

GRATITUDE MORNING

Before you begin your day, list 10 things you´re grateful for.

_____
_____
_____
_____
_____
_____
_____
_____
_____
_____

WHAT I´M LEARNING FROM MY CHALLENGES

List three obstacles and what you´re learning from them.

1 What I´m learning:

2 What I´m learning:

3 What I´m learning:

PEOPLE I´M GRATEFUL FOR

List 5 people who made your life a little happier today. these could be friends, family or strangers.

_____
_____
_____
_____
_____

THE BEST PART OF MY DAY

Choose one moment of your day that made you happy and focus on it for 5 minutes before bed.

_____
_____
_____
_____
_____
_____
_____
_____

Date: / /

GRATITUDE JOURNAL

GRATITUDE MORNING
Before you begin your day, list 10 things you´re grateful for.

1 _____
2 _____
3 _____
4 _____
5 _____
6 _____
7 _____
8 _____
9 _____
10_____

WHAT I´M LEARNING FROM MY CHALLENGES
List three obstacles and what you´re learning from them.

1 What I´m learning:

2 What I´m learning:

3 What I´m learning:

PEOPLE I´M GRATEFUL FOR
List 5 people who made your life a little happier today. these could be friends, family or strangers.

1 _____
2 _____
3 _____
4 _____
5 _____

THE BEST PART OF MY DAY
Choose one moment of your day that made you happy and focus on it for 5 minutes before bed.

_____
_____
_____
_____
_____
_____
_____
_____

Date: / /

GRATITUDE JOURNAL

GRATITUDE MORNING

Before you begin your day, list 10 things you´re grateful for.

_____
_____
_____
_____
_____
_____
_____
_____
_____
_____
_____
_____
_____

WHAT I´M LEARNING FROM MY CHALLENGES

List three obstacles and what you´re learning from them.

1 What I´m learning:

2 What I´m learning:

3 What I´m learning:

PEOPLE I´M GRATEFUL FOR

List 5 people who made your life a little happier today. these could be friends, family or strangers.

_____
_____
_____
_____
_____

THE BEST PART OF MY DAY

Choose one moment of your day that made you happy and focus on it for 5 minutes before bed.

_____
_____
_____
_____
_____
_____
_____
_____

Date: / /

GRATITUDE JOURNAL

GRATITUDE MORNING
Before you begin your day, list 10 things you´re grateful for.

1 _____
2 _____
3 _____
4 _____
5 _____
6 _____
7 _____
8 _____
9 _____
10 _____

WHAT I´M LEARNING FROM MY CHALLENGES
List three obstacles and what you´re learning from them.

1 What I´m learning:

2 What I´m learning:

3 What I´m learning:

PEOPLE I´M GRATEFUL FOR
List 5 people who made your life a little happier today. these could be friends, family or strangers.

1 _____
2 _____
3 _____
4 _____
5 _____

THE BEST PART OF MY DAY
Choose one moment of your day that made you happy and focus on it for 5 minutes before bed.

_____
_____
_____
_____
_____
_____
_____
_____
_____

Date: / /

GRATITUDE JOURNAL

GRATITUDE MORNING

Before you begin your day, list 10 things you´re grateful for.

_____
_____
_____
_____
_____
_____
_____
_____
_____
_____
_____
_____
_____

WHAT I´M LEARNING FROM MY CHALLENGES

List three obstacles and what you´re learning from them.

1 What I´m learning:

2 What I´m learning:

3 What I´m learning:

PEOPLE I´M GRATEFUL FOR

List 5 people who made your life a little happier today. these could be friends, family or strangers.

_____
_____
_____
_____
_____
_____

THE BEST PART OF MY DAY

Choose one moment of your day that made you happy and focus on it for 5 minutes before bed.

_____
_____
_____
_____
_____
_____
_____
_____

My Mood Tracker

Month

Today I Felt...

31 1 2 3 4 5 6 7 8 9 10 11 12 13 14 15 16 17 18 19 20 21 22 23 24 25 26 27 28 29 30

Energetic/Motivated

Happy

Content/Neutral

Sad

Anxious

Irritable/Annoyed

Angry

Sick/Tired

SUCCESS

HARD WORK
PERSISTENCE
LATE NIGHTS
REJECTION
SACRIFICES
DISCIPLINE
CRITICISM
DOUBTS
FAILURES
RISKS
NEVER GIVE UP!

THE NOT-TO-DO LIST

EVERYTHING ON MY PLATE

OTHER PEOPLE'S RESPONSIBILITIES

STUFF THAT'S OUT OF MY CONTROL

STUFF THAT DRAINS ME

GET IT DONE

Date:

TODAY OR ELSE

_____
_____
_____
_____
_____
_____
_____
_____
_____

ASAP

_____
_____
_____
_____
_____
_____
_____
_____
_____

SOONER OR LATER

_____
_____
_____
_____
_____
_____
_____
_____
_____

THIS MORNING

_____
_____
_____
_____
_____
_____
_____
_____
_____

THIS AFTERNOON

_____
_____
_____
_____
_____
_____
_____
_____
_____

THIS EVENING

_____
_____
_____
_____
_____
_____
_____
_____
_____

TOMORROW

_____
_____
_____
_____
_____
_____
_____
_____
_____
_____
_____

NOTES

_____
_____
_____
_____
_____
_____
_____
_____
_____
_____

PROJECTS AND EXAMS

Description   Deadline

Class   Important Days
_____   _____
                                              _____
Details   _____
_____   _____
_____
_____   Complete

Description   Deadline

Class   Important Days
_____   _____
                                              _____
Details   _____
_____   _____
_____
_____   Complete

Description   Deadline

Class   Important Days
_____   _____
                                              _____
Details   _____
_____   _____
_____
_____   Complete

HOMEWORK

TO DO LIST

MONDAY

_____
_____
_____
_____

TUESDAY

_____
_____
_____
_____
_____

WEDNESDAY

_____
_____
_____
_____

REMINDERS

THURSDAY

_____
_____
_____
_____

FRIDAY

_____
_____
_____

My Mood Tracker

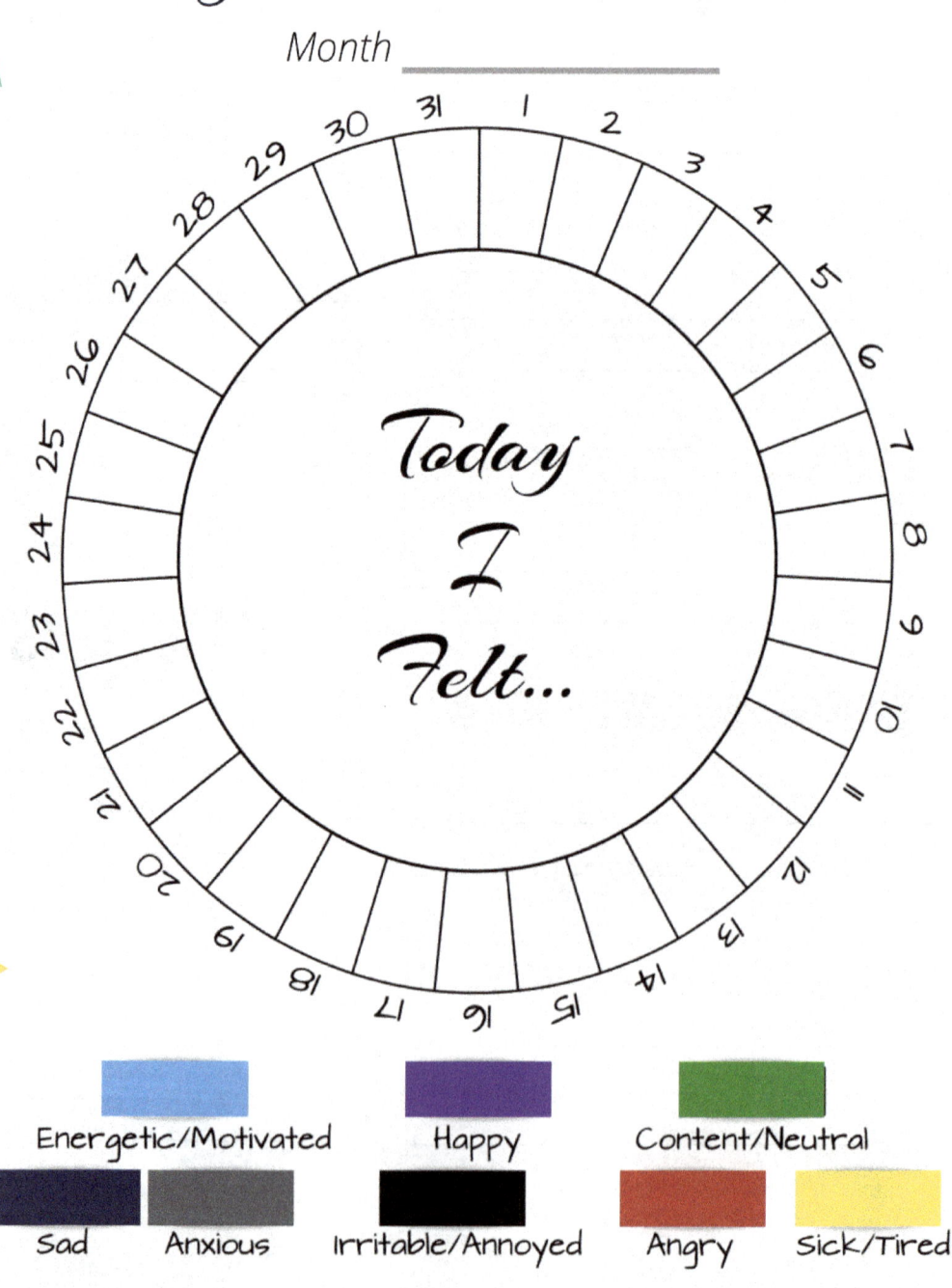

Month _____

Today I Felt...

(Calendar wheel numbered 1–31 around the circle)

Energetic/Motivated · **Happy** · **Content/Neutral**

Sad · **Anxious** · **Irritable/Annoyed** · **Angry** · **Sick/Tired**

TODAY IS: _____

6:00	
7:00	
8:00	
9:00	
10:00	
11:00	
12:00	
1:00	
2:00	
3:00	
4:00	
5:00	
6:00	
7:00	
8:00	
9:00	

ASSIGNMENTS

CHORES

NOTES

NOTES

WEEKLY PLANNER

Monday

Tuesday

Wednesday

Thursday

Friday

Sat/Sun

WEEKLY PLANNER

Monday

Tuesday

Wednesday

Thursday

Friday

Sat/Sun

WEEKLY PLANNER

Monday

Tuesday

Wednesday

Thursday

Friday

Sat/Sun

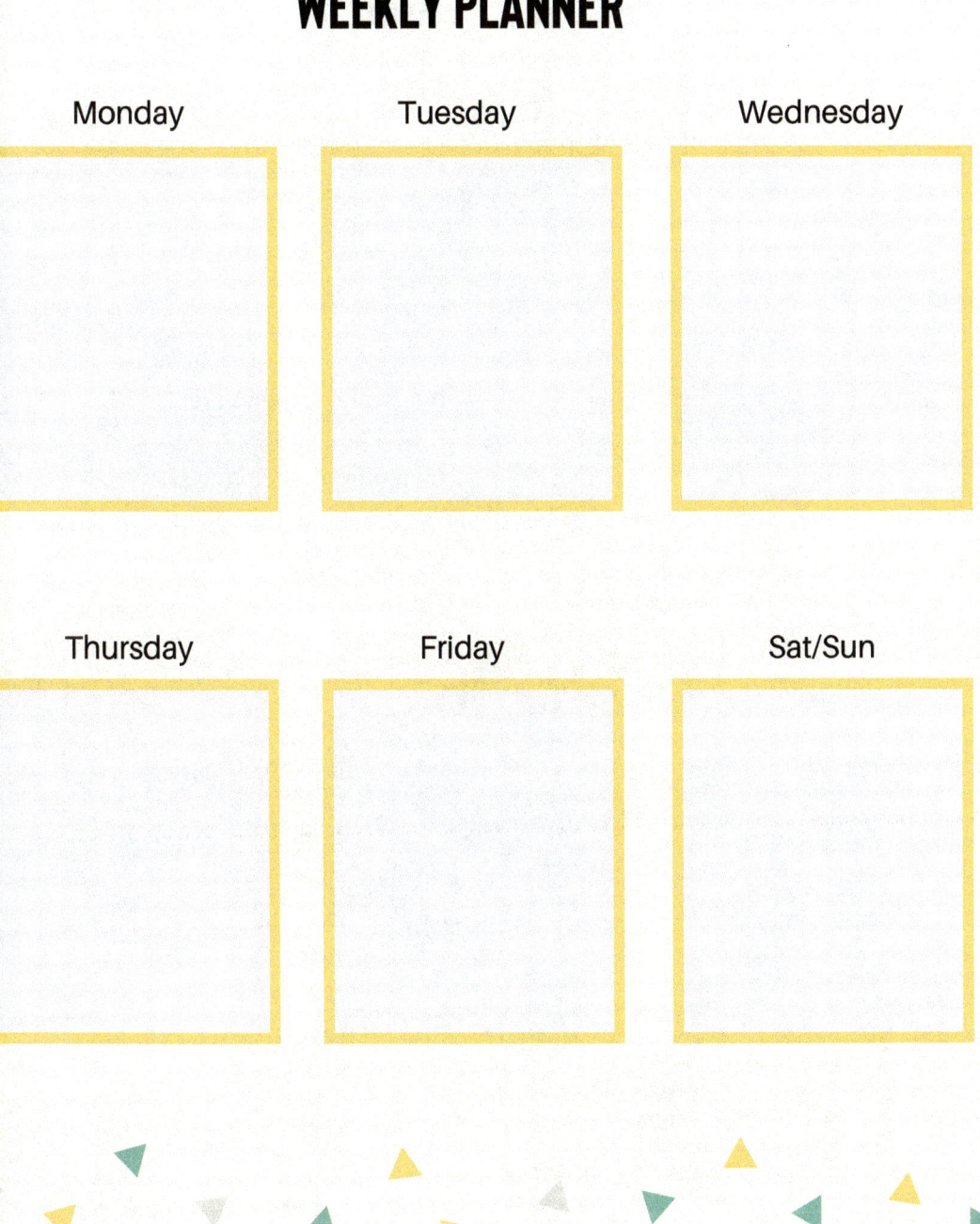

WEEKLY PLANNER

Monday

Tuesday

Wednesday

Thursday

Friday

Sat/Sun

WEEKLY PLANNER

Monday

Tuesday

Wednesday

Thursday

Friday

Sat/Sun

WEEKLY PLANNER

Monday

Tuesday

Wednesday

Thursday

Friday

Sat/Sun

WEEKLY PLANNER

Monday

Tuesday

Wednesday

Thursday

Friday

Sat/Sun

WEEKLY PLANNER

Monday

Tuesday

Wednesday

Thursday

Friday

Sat/Sun

WEEKLY PLANNER

Monday

Tuesday

Wednesday

Thursday

Friday

Sat/Sun

WEEKLY PLANNER

Monday

Tuesday

Wednesday

Thursday

Friday

Sat/Sun

WEEKLY PLANNER

Monday

Tuesday

Wednesday

Thursday

Friday

Sat/Sun

WEEKLY PLANNER

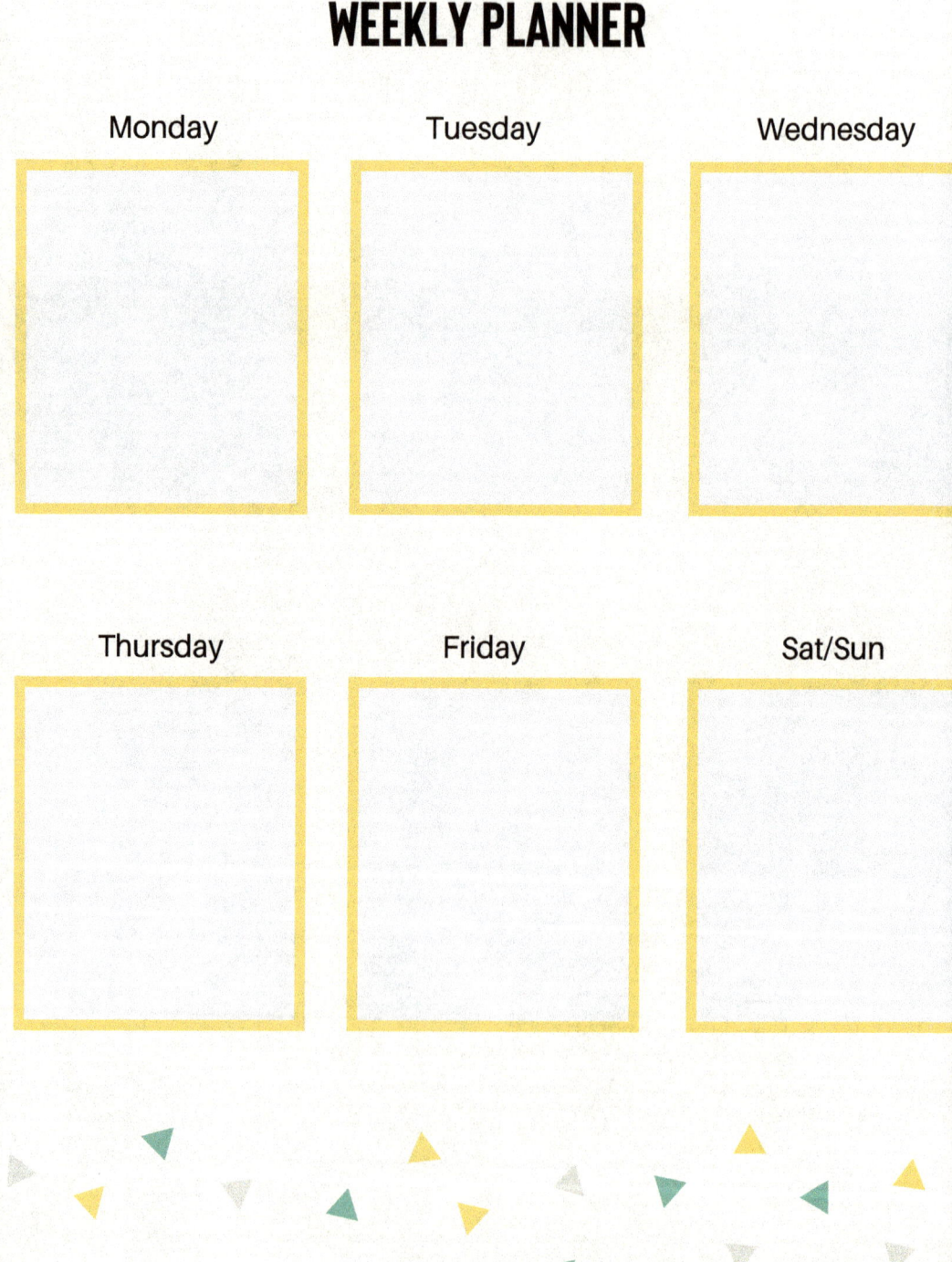

Monday	Tuesday	Wednesday

Thursday	Friday	Sat/Sun

What's on my mind? ..

Date: / /

_____
_____
_____
_____
_____
_____
_____
_____
_____
_____
_____
_____
_____
_____
_____
_____
_____
_____
_____
_____

What's on my mind?

Date: / /

What's on my mind? ..

Date: / /

_____
_____
_____
_____
_____
_____
_____
_____
_____
_____
_____
_____
_____
_____
_____
_____
_____
_____
_____
_____
_____
_____

What's on my mind?

What's on my mind? ..

Date: / /

What's on my mind?

Date: / /

_____

_____

_____

_____

_____

_____

_____

_____

_____

_____

_____

_____

_____

_____

_____

_____

_____

_____

_____

_____

What's on my mind? ..•

Date: / /

_____
_____
_____
_____
_____
_____
_____
_____
_____
_____
_____
_____
_____
_____
_____
_____
_____
_____
_____
_____
_____

What's on my mind?

Date: / /

_____
_____
_____
_____
_____
_____
_____
_____
_____
_____
_____
_____
_____
_____
_____
_____
_____
_____

What's on my mind? ..

What's on my mind?

Date: / /

_____
_____
_____
_____
_____
_____
_____
_____
_____
_____
_____
_____
_____
_____
_____
_____
_____
_____

NOTES

NOTES

NOTES

NOTES

NOTES

NOTES

CPSIA information can be obtained
at www.ICGtesting.com
Printed in the USA
BVHW051322130120
569376BV00009B/456/P

9 781087 858845